The Cat in the Hat's Learning Library

The Cat in the Hat's Learning Library

The Cat in the Hat's Learning Library

The Cat in the Hat's Learning Library

The Cat in the Hat's Learning Library

The Cat in the Hat's Learning Library

The Cat in the Hat's Learning Library

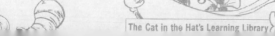

The Cat in the Hat's Learning Library

The editors would like to thank
BARBARA KIEFER, Ph.D.,
Charlotte S. Huck Professor of Children's Literature,
The Ohio State University, and
SARAH MORGAN, National Examiner,
United States Pony Club,
for their assistance in the preparation of this book.

Visit us on the Web!
Seussville.com
randomhousekids.com

Educators and librarians, for a variety of teaching tools, visit us at
RHTeachersLibrarians.com

Library of Congress Cataloging-in-Publication Data
Worth, Bonnie.
If I ran the horse show : all about horses / by Bonnie Worth ; illustrated by Aristides Ruiz and
Joe Mathieu. — 1st ed.
   p. cm. — (The Cat in the Hat's learning library)
Includes bibliographical references and index.
ISBN 978-0-375-86683-8 (trade) — ISBN 978-0-375-96683-5 (lib. bdg.)
1. Horses—Juvenile literature. I. Ruiz, Aristides, ill. II. Mathieu, Joseph, ill. III. Title.
SF302.W67 2012   636.1—dc23   2011024236

Printed in the United States of America   25 24 23 22 21 20 19 18 17 16 15

If I Ran the Horse Show

by Bonnie Worth

illustrated by Aristides Ruiz and Joe Mathieu

The Cat in the Hat's Learning Library®

Random House 🏠 New York

I'm the Cat in the Hat!
And today we will go
to my Super-Tremendous
Stupendous Horse Show!

But I warn you, I might
get a little bit sappy.
When it comes to horses,
I get really happy!

Horses and people
have long worked as one.
They've formed a strong bond,
when all's said and done.

Horses were hunted
by cavemen as prey.

Farmers learned later
to make them obey.

All horses are treated
(you will find this fact fun)
as if they were born
on January one.

JAN.
1

A foal is a horse who
is less than one year.
A yearling (surprise!)
is a year—is that clear?

MARE / DAM

FOAL

A filly's a female
who is less than four.
A mare is a female
who's four years or more.

A colt is a male horse
who is less than four.
A stallion's a male
who's four years or more.

A dam is a horse
who is also a mama.
A sire is a stallion,
a horse's papa.

STALLION/SIRE

YEARLING

Gelding is the word
that people use for
a male who can't
make foals anymore.

GELDING

Before we go on,
it is good, I suppose,
to look at a horse
from its tail to its nose.

The top of the tail is
what we call the dock.
Then haunch and stifle
and gaskin and hock.
Hip, loins, back, flank,
withers, poll, crest.

Now take a deep breath
and go on with the rest.
Neck, jaw, and chin groove,
forehead and foretop,
nostril and muzzle—
is it time to stop?

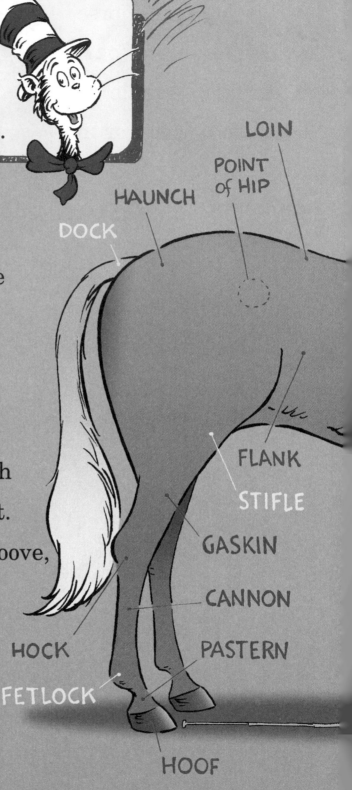

LOIN

POINT of HIP

HAUNCH

DOCK

FLANK

STIFLE

GASKIN

CANNON

PASTERN

HOCK

FETLOCK

HOOF

POLL
FORETOP
CREST
FOREHEAD
NECK
MUZZLE
NOSTRIL
WITHERS
JAW
BACK
CHIN GROOVE
POINT of SHOULDER
CHEST
FOREARM
ELBOW
KNEE
CORONET

No! Our look at the horse
can't be rated complete
until we have looked at
the legs and the feet.

Hoof, coronet, pastern,
knee and fetlock,
elbow and cannon,
then back to the hock!

Nerves under horsehide
can feel a fly creeping.
A tail fends off flies
by swatting and sweeping.

RIGHT EYE

BOTH
EYES

LEFT EYE

Eyes set on the side,

as with all those that are prey,
see predators coming
from far, far away.

Legs made for running
help horses to hie.
Flat hooves keep them steady
on wet turf or dry.

Most horses we ride—
this will not be big news—
have hooves that are guarded
by strong iron shoes.

Horse hooves, like your nails,
are made up of stuff
that doesn't have feeling.
Oh, hoof stuff is tough!

A farrier trims
horses' hooves with a file.
Horses should have this done
every once in a while.

He heats up horseshoes
until they are hot,
then nails them on tight.
Does it hurt? It does not!

Horses step out, or move,
at a number of rates.

Walk,  trot,

canter,  gallop—

we call these steps gaits.

Standardbred horses
can move at a pace,
a fast gait they use
when they run in a race.

The Icelandic pony
has what's called a tolt,
a swift gait that's smooth,
with nary a jolt.

Both Standard and Icy,
these two that you see,
are what we call breeds.
What are breeds? you ask me.

They are horses who mix
with similar mates
and give birth to foals
who have the same traits.

This breed is a Clydesdale.

It's bred to be big.

The Falabella is as small

as a six-month-old pig.

The Clydesdale, we know,
measures eighteen hands high.
The Falabella is seven.
What a cute little guy!

A hand is four inches.
It equals the span
of a hand that belongs
to a fully grown man.

We start from the ground
and then measure till we
get up to the withers—
no higher. You see?

Quarter horse is a breed
that started out West.
It's easy to handle and
herds cows the best.

Appaloosas are horses
that are covered with spots.
Native Americans liked
this spotted breed lots.

In the sandy Sahara
the Arabian's a prize.
It has grace and speed
and a delicate size.

It can do with less water
in dry desert lands
and runs without sinking
deep into desert sands.

Arabians now live
the whole world round.
Where there are horse lovers,
this breed can be found.

With large eyes and nostrils
and a dainty muzzle,
it's easy to handle
and happy to nuzzle.

The Fjord (FEE-ord), from Norway,
can deal with rough weather.
They say it is stronger
than good, tough shoe leather.

Australian stock horses—
sometimes called Walers—
came Down Under with British
settlers and sailors.

Connemara ponies go
on great riding tours
of Ireland's fair marshes
and its rolling moors.

These hunters and jumpers—
so the story goes—
swam from Spanish shipwrecks.
But who really knows!

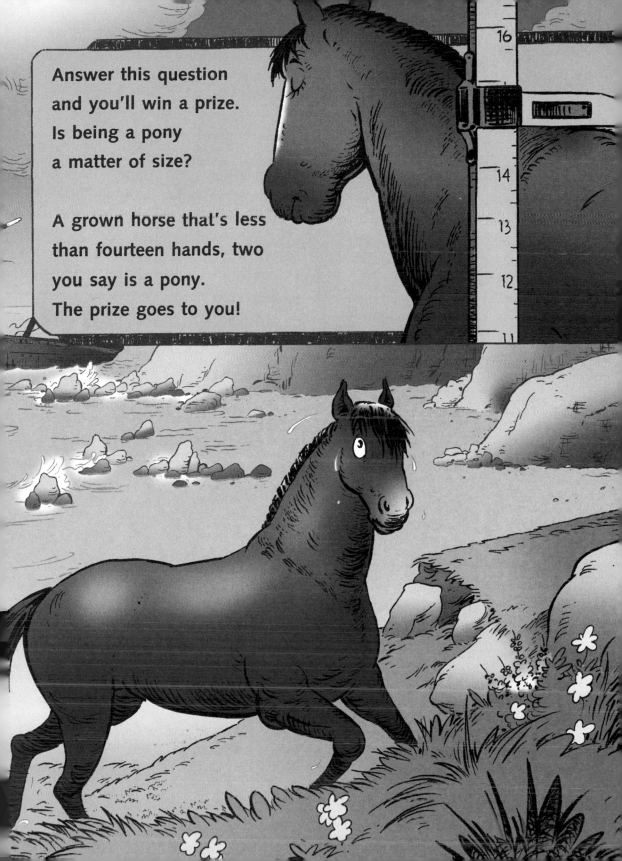

Answer this question
and you'll win a prize.
Is being a pony
a matter of size?

A grown horse that's less
than fourteen hands, two
you say is a pony.
The prize goes to you!

The Lipizzan horse
from the Spanish Riding School
can dance and prance nimbly—
so elegant and cool!

A Lipizzan's proud,
with a beautiful mane,
crossbred from Arabians
and horses from Spain.

The school is in Austria
and has won worldwide fame.
Its half-Spanish horses
inspired the school's name.

The Morgan is smart
and learns quickly how
to pull rigs, plow the fields,
run a race, herd a cow.

Thoroughbred is a horse
born and bred for the track.
It carries a jockey
upon its sleek back.

It runs in big races
of worldwide renown
like the Ascot, the Epsom,
and the Triple Crown.

Mustangs roam wild
on the wide-open plains.
They've never known saddles
or the feel of the reins.

Bit, reins, and saddle
are what we call tack.
Reins and bit on the head,
saddle over the back.

BIT

HEADSTALL

CANTLE

HORN

POMMEL

JOCKEY

CHIN
STRAP

GULLET

SEAT

REAR
JOCKEY

REINS

LATIGO
KEEPER

SKIRT

LATIGO

CINCH
RING

STIRRUP
LEATHER

STIRRUP

CINCH

WESTERN

There are western saddles
and the English kind.
The difference between them
let us bear in mind.

BROWBAND

HEADSTALL

CHEEK PIECE

NOSEBAND

THROATLATCH

CANTLE

POMMEL

GULLET

SEAT

REINS

BIT

FLAP

GIRTH

LEATHERS

STIRRUP IRON

ENGLISH

Western is made

for the cowboy's long haul.

English is for hunting and

jumping and all.

On English, we post
and we must learn the knack
of rising up off of
the trotting horse back.

We stick to the western
and we do not rise.
Either English or western
is great exercise!

Now put on the saddle,
the reins, and the bit.
Your hard riding cap—
you can't forget it!

The judges are waiting.
It's time for the show.
So pick up the reins . . .

. . . giddyup and let's go!

GLOSSARY

Down Under: A term used for Australia, which is "down under" the equator.

Farrier: A person trained to put shoes on horses.

Hie: To go quickly.

Inspired: Filled with the spirit to do something.

Jockey: A person who rides a racehorse.

Knack: A special ability.

Moor: Grassy, wind-swept land with few trees.

Nary a: Another way of saying "not one."

Nimbly: Lightly and quickly.

Post: To rise and fall with the movement of a trotting horse.

Predator: A hunter.

Prey: An animal that is hunted.

Trait: An inherited quality.

FOR FURTHER READING

The Girl Who Loved Wild Horses by Paul Goble (Richard Jackson Books). A Caldecott Award–winning folktale about a Native American girl's love of horses. For ages 4–8.

Horse by Juliet Clutton-Brock (DK Publishing, *DK Eyewitness Books*). All about horses—their history, anatomy, and breeds and the many different jobs they do. For grades 3 and up.

Horse Heroes: True Stories of Amazing Horses by Kate Petty (DK Publishing, *DK Readers,* Level 4). Famous horses throughout history. For grades 3–5.

Horse Song: The Naadam of Mongolia by Ted and Betsy Lewin (Lee & Low Books, *Adventures Around the World*). The story of a young boy who rides his horse for the first time in Naadam, the Mongolian summer festival. For grades 2–5.

Horses by Seymour Simon (HarperCollins). An NSTA-CBC Outstanding Science Trade Book for Children, containing full-color maps, photographs, and diagrams of horses. For kindergarten and up.

Judy Richter's Riding for Kids (Storey Publishing). An introduction to horsemanship by a highly regarded instructor. For ages 9–12.

INDEX

Appaloosas, 23
Arabians, 24–25, 30
Australian stock horses, 27

back, 12
bit, 34, 38

cannons, 13
canter, 18
cavemen, 9
chin groove, 12
Clydesdales, 20–21
colts, 11
Connemara ponies, 28
coronets, 13
cowboys, 36
crest, 12

dams, 11
dock, 12

elbows, 13
English riding, 35–37
eyes, 14, 25

Falabellas, 20–21
farmers, 9

farriers, 16–17
fetlocks, 13
fillies, 10
Fjords, 26
flanks, 12
foals, 10, 11, 19
forehead, 12
foretop, 12

gaits, 18–19
gallop, 18
gaskins, 12
geldings, 11

hands, 21, 29
haunches, 12
hips, 12
hocks, 12, 13
hooves, 13, 15–17
horses
    birthday of, 10
    breeds of, 19–33
    measuring, 21, 29
    parts of, 12–15
    people and, 8–9
horseshoes, 15–17

Icelandic ponies, 19

jaw, 12

knees, 13

legs, 13, 15
Lipizzans, 30
loins, 12

mares, 10
Morgans, 31
mustangs, 33
muzzle, 12, 25

Native Americans, 23
neck, 12
nerves, 14
nostrils, 12, 25

pasterns, 13
poll, 12
ponies, 19, 28, 29

quarter horses, 22

racing, 32
reins, 33, 34, 38, 39

saddle, 33, 34, 38

sires, 11
Spanish Riding School, 30
stallions, 11
Standardbreds, 18
stifles, 12

tack, 34–35, 38
tail, 12, 14
Thoroughbreds, 32
tolt, 19
trot, 18, 37

Walers, 27
walk, 18
western riding, 34–37
withers, 12, 21

yearlings, 10